Counting Money

By Julie Dalton

Consultant
Ari Ginsburg
Math Curriculum Specialist

Children's Press®
A Division of Scholastic Inc.
New York   Toronto   London   Auckland   Sydney
Mexico City   New Delhi   Hong Kong
Danbury, Connecticut

Designer: Herman Adler Design
Photo Researcher: Caroline Anderson
The photo on the cover shows a boy thinking about counting the money
in his piggy bank.

Library of Congress Cataloging-in-Publication Data

Dalton, Julie, 1951–
  Counting money / by Julie Dalton.
      p. cm. — (Rookie read-about math)
  Includes index.
  ISBN 0-516-25260-7 (lib. bdg.)   0-516-25361-1 (pbk.)
  1. Counting—Juvenile literature. 2. Money—Juvenile literature. I. Title.
II. Series.
  QA113.D357 2005
  513.2'11—dc22   2005004032

CHILDREN'S PRESS, and ROOKIE READ-ABOUT®,
and associated logos are trademarks and/or registered trademarks
of Scholastic Library Publishing. SCHOLASTIC and associated logos
are trademarks and/or registered trademarks of Scholastic Inc.

1 2 3 4 5 6 7 8 9 10 R 14 13 12 11 10 09 08 07 06 05

Ben wants to count his coins.

4

Can you guess what
he does?

Ben shakes out all the
coins. He makes piles
of coins.

He makes a pile of
pennies, a pile of nickels,
a pile of dimes, and a pile
of quarters.

Pennies look like this. One penny equals one cent.

The symbol for the word cent is $\cent$.

A symbol is something that stands for something else.

1 penny = 1¢

Ben counts the pennies.
He counts by ones.
1, 2, 3, 4, 5, 6, 7, 8, 9, 10.

Ten pennies equal ten
cents. He writes it like
this: 10¢.

Nickels look like this. One
nickel equals five cents.

1 nickel = 5¢

Five pennies equal one nickel.

5 pennies = 1 nickel

Ben counts his nickels.
He counts by fives.
5, 10, 15, 20, 25, 30, 35, 40.

Eight nickels equal forty
cents. He writes it like
this: 40¢.

Dimes look like this. One dime equals ten cents.

1 dime = 10¢

Ten pennies equal one dime.
Two nickels equal one dime.

10 pennies = 1 dime

2 nickels = 1 dime

Ben counts his dimes.
He counts by tens.
10, 20, 30, 40, 50, 60.

Six dimes equal sixty
cents. He writes it like
this: 60¢.

Quarters look like this.
One quarter equals
twenty-five cents.

1 quarter = 25¢

Twenty-five pennies equal
one quarter. Five nickels
equal one quarter.

25 pennies = 25¢

5 nickels = 25¢

Ben counts the quarters.
He counts by 25s.
25, 50, 75.

Three quarters equal
seventy-five cents. He
writes it like this: 75¢.

22

Ben wants to play a game.

He puts all the coins into one pile.

He closes his eyes and picks out three coins.

Ben opens his eyes.

He sees two dimes and one nickel in his hand.

How much do they equal?

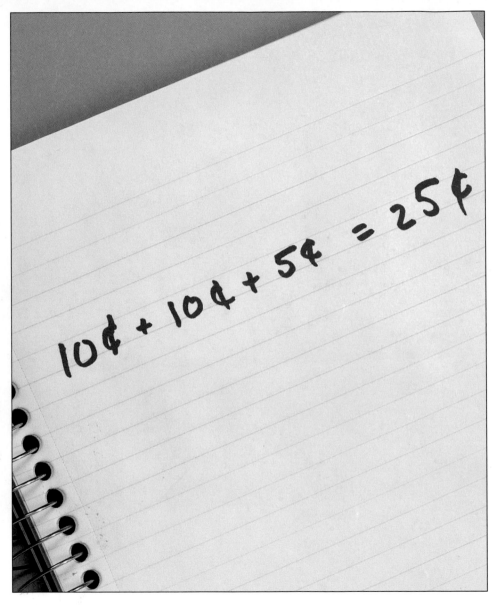

Did you get the right answer?

What is that sound?

An ice-cream truck is coming! Ben grabs all the coins and runs.

Counting coins is fun!

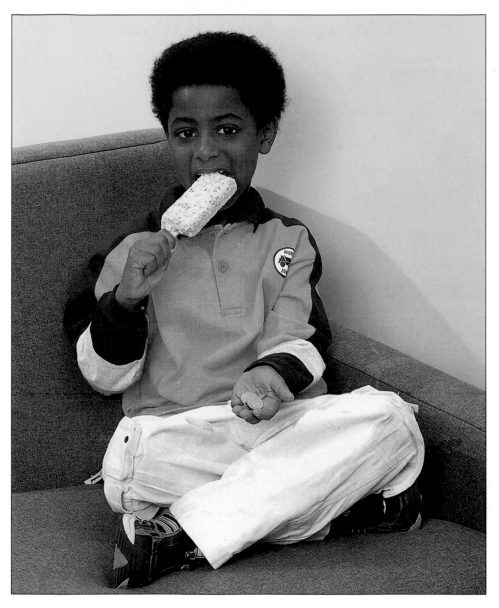

Words You Know

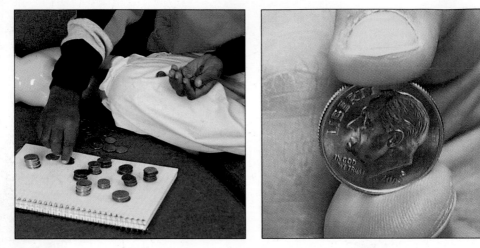

coins

dime

ice cream

nickel

penny

quarter

Index

cents (¢), 5, 9, 10, 13, 14, 16, 18, 20

dimes, 5, 14, 15–16, 24

game, 23–24, 27

ice cream, 27

nickels, 5, 10, 11, 13, 15, 19, 24

pennies, 5, 6–7, 9, 11, 15, 19

piles of coins, 5

quarters, 5, 18, 19–20

symbols, 6

About the Author

Julie Dalton is an editor and writer who lives in central Connecticut. She lives with her big hairy dog, a gentle cat, and several teenagers.

Photo Credits

10/06